D1742960

Live Organised

A practical guide to

an organised life

Marcia Francois

MARCIA FRANCOIS

ISBN-10: 1467958107
ISBN-13: 978-1467958103

Dedication

To Pastor Peter Cox, who believed in me and my
message long before I ever did.

TESTIMONIALS

Marcia is the expert on helping you have the time and freedom to thrive. Now you can have her help you 24/7 in her new book Live Organised.

If you're ready for powerful change, this book is for you.

Elizabeth Hagen

Author of *Organize with Confidence* and *Confidence: Now is Your Time*

www.TheConfidenceBook.com

Marcia Francois truly is the Organising Queen.

If you need a starting place – or a re-starting place – for your organising journey, Marcia's book is the place to start.

Jill Hart
Christian Work at Home Moms

www.cwahm.com

Contents

Introduction
My story   **4**

Why do you want to get organised?   **8**

Part 1
Overcoming disorder

Seven myths about organising   **10**
Get your mindset in gear   **15**
The most common organising question ever **18**

Part 2
Let's get organised

My organising approach   **23**

1. It's not a once-off activity
2. Organising just enough
3. Your individual organising style

Three parts to getting and staying organised **33**

1. Motivation
2. Skills
3. Accountability and support

My DREAM method of organising any space **40**

My favourite organising principles   **66**

Set up your routines for success   **72**

Part 3
Beyond getting organised

Avoid these organising mistakes   **75**
Green organising   **77**
In closing   **81**

Part 4
15 Tools to organise your home and life   **82**

1. My future organised home

2. Plan your attack

3. Master to do list

4. Projects to do in 15 minutes

5. Projects to do in 1 hour

6. My routines

7. Grocery list

8. Goals form – category

9. Goals form – blank

10. Eat the frog

11. Monthly planner

12. Monthly menu planner

13. Priority list

14. Health chart

15. Travel checklist

15. Acknowledgments

Thank you to my husband, Dion, for always being a support and encouragement to me.

Thank you to my babies, Kendra and Connor, for inspiring me to take those little gifts of time and make something out of them.

And most of all, thank you to my Lord and Saviour, Jesus Christ, for giving me these gifts to share with the world.

MY STORY

Hi, I'm Marcia.

I've always been relatively organised but I must confess something – it's because I'm really lazy and I enjoy having lots of time for sleeping and reading.

So I try and set up things well at the start to save me time down the line.

My "system" has worked for me all these years (at the time of writing this book, I've been married for nearly 17 years) and worked even better for me the last three years since I had my twins.

As any mother knows, once babies enter the picture, the visions of a totally neat and organised home go out the window and you really have to choose how to best spend your time.

The strange thing is that I grew up in a home that was not organised – we ran out of things often, meals were never planned and we shopped on the spur of the moment – this may have been the reason I run my own home so differently.

It didn't all happen at once though.

We got into a weekly shopping routine quite quickly and I had a fairly organised home but two things happened that made me realise I could do much, much better.

1. We had a burglary at our home and when the insurance assessor came to check the damage, he thought there were FOUR people living in our house and not just the two of us.

I was horrified and slightly embarrassed.

Yes, our things were organised but we had way too much.

2. We eventually sold that house and bought another.

As I started packing and packing, and still packing some more, I realised that we still had far too much stuff.

We then started decluttering but even once we'd moved into the new house, we were decluttering a box a week, easily.

I think I had about 20 boxes just for the kitchen and we found that when everything was unpacked, we had about four or five boxes left.

I decided then that the house didn't have enough storage space and brought in builders to give me quotes to put up more cabinets in the kitchen.

When I found out how much one half wall of cabinets would cost, I promptly abandoned that idea and decided to declutter all those boxes instead.

And that's really when my true, consistent journey to a simplified and organised life began.

I don't have all the answers but I have practised everything I talk about in this book over and over and over through the years, and the principles do work.

I'm also a professional organiser who has helped hundreds of people over the years declutter their homes and businesses, and get and stay organised.

My prayer is that you'll be the next one.

Love and organising success

Marcia Francois

1. WHY DO YOU WANT TO GET ORGANISED?

You've probably picked up this book because you feel frustrated, overwhelmed or stressed at the disorder in your life.

You know there has to be a better way to get your life in order so that you can start living again.

My job is to show you how to go from chaos to order in the quickest and easiest way possible.

Shall we begin?

Part 1

Overcoming disorder

2. SEVEN MYTHS ABOUT ORGANISING

Myth 1: You're either born organised or you're not

Yes, some people do tend to be naturally more organised but we now know that organising is a skill that can be learnt.

Myth 2: Organising is expensive

It can be expensive if you let it. I prefer not to let it get expensive because I don't think it's necessary.

If you can afford to spend a little more money to get visually appealing containers for items that are out in the open, go ahead, but for containers in closed cupboards or shelving, it really isn't necessary.

Repurpose things. It's better for the environment, it's better on your pocket and it will give you a sense of fulfillment as you get creative.

Myth 3: One size fits all organising

It's important to identify your own organising style (we'll figure yours out later) so that you implement systems that work for you and your family.

I can't function in an environment where too much is out in the open but maybe you can't function if you can't see your things.

Figure out your style and embrace it.

Myth 4: Once you get organised, it stays that way

We'll deal with this myth later but for now know that organising is a continual process. Even your systems need constant tweaking as your life changes.

Myth 5: You need huge blocks of time to get organised

Not true.

Quite honestly, I don't know anybody who has huge blocks of time to get organised.

During my twin pregnancy, and especially for the first 12 and again from 23 weeks onward, I was exhausted. I could barely stand and cook a meal for 30 minutes. During that time it was down to the basics – eating, getting dressed, going to work and sleeping.

I didn't have a lot of time for organising so while the kettle was boiling for my cup of coffee, I would quickly organise a cabinet for 2 minutes. While I was cooking, I would see what else I could do in the kitchen or in the laundry area.

That's often the way we have to do things, especially as mothers. You don't need 3 hours to get something organised; all you need is 5, 10 or 15 minutes at a time, whatever suits your lifestyle.

Myth 6: There's a right way and a wrong way to get organised

While I like to think my way is the best way to get organised, I know that's not true. You should also be aware that while each of the principles I'm discussing in this book have and will work for hundreds of people, they may not all work for you.

That's okay. Take what works for you and leave the rest.

My personal guideline with anything I do is that if it saves me just 10 minutes a day, it's been worthwhile.

Remember 10 minutes a day equals 60 hours over the course of a year.

Myth 7: If it's not pretty, it's not organised

I blame this myth on television, blogs and now Pinterest. Somehow we've all started believing that for a space to be organised it's got to be cute and pretty.

That's not true.

Of course it may help you keep the space organised if you make it pretty to start with but that is not a requirement.

Organised is one thing and pretty is another.

I've seen some beautiful spaces that were totally disorganised and again, not the cutest spaces on earth but they were organised and functioned well for the family in question.

3. GET YOUR MINDSET IN GEAR

Before we get into the practical aspects of organising, let's pause for a moment and talk about the mental side of organising.

There are three things we need to talk about: perfectionism, perseverance and attitude.

Perfectionism is not the goal

Would it surprise you to know that many perfectionists live in cluttered and disorganised homes?

It's true.

That's because they've bought into the all or nothing mentality.

"If I can't do something perfectly, I'd better not do it at all".

If this is you, start challenging yourself to do something about your situation, even if imperfectly. It doesn't matter if you don't have enough time, storage containers or all the know-how.

Just start.

Persevere with it

Some people get frustrated when the organising process doesn't magically transform their homes as they imagined it would get done, like in an afternoon or a day.

Please remember to persevere – it always looks worse before it gets better.

I feel like I need to warn you of obstacles so that you don't think you "just don't have it in you" when it seems like it's never going to come together.

It will – be patient and persevere.

Keep a positive attitude

If you're going to get and stay organised, you need to have a good attitude.

Organising is not a once-off affair.

You'll organise a space, tweak, tweak and tweak some more until it works perfectly for your family, and then something changes – you move, your kids move into a different stage and you have to re-organise again.

This is life.

It helps to have a positive attitude when your family doesn't abide by your organising rules or mess up your systems.

Always remember what Suze Orman says: people first and then things.

4. THE MOST COMMON ORGANISING QUESTION EVER

Marcia, I want to get organised but it's all so overwhelming.

Where on earth do I start?

There are different ways to approach this question but before we even start with the practical aspects, you need to do this:

First of all, relax and take a deep breath :-)

Then get your mind in the right space.

Now that we've got that part settled, let's talk practically.

Do you want to make the biggest impact first or do you want a quick win?

Either

1. Start with the area of your home or life that bothers you the most.

If you can't bear to choose clothes every morning because your wardrobe is too cluttered, then that's probably a good place to start.

If you find yourself tossing and turning because of the state of your home, then start with an area of great impact.

The benefit of choosing the area of most frustration is that you're going to start feeling better about your home almost immediately.

This approach is usually best for those who are in the **all or nothing** camp. You like to get in there, tackle it all and it's done.

Or

2. Start with a smaller area where you can get a quick win.

While you're getting the hang of organising, you may want to choose a small space like your desktop, a junk drawer or a bedside table.

This will enable you to practise the principles and hone your skills for the bigger areas of your home.

The small space also works best when you only have a limited amount of time but you want to get started anyway.

For example, if you have little children like I do, you're not going to find huge gaps of time to organise so take the slivers of time you find here and there. There's a form at the back of the book called "Projects to do in 15 minutes" which is meant for exactly this purpose.

So, where do *you* think you should start?

Part 2

Let's get organised

5. MY ORGANISING APPROACH

In my years of working with clients and writing the blog at http://www.OrganisingQueen.com, you'll find that I emphasise three things a lot.

This is what I believe with all my heart and is the reason I'm going to take up some time now to lay the foundation, because it's that important.

1. Organising is not a once-off activity

If you think once you get organised that's the end of the story you're going to be very disappointed. ☺

Organising is a journey. There is always going to be adjusting, tweaking, maintaining and redoing because our lives are always changing.

For example, before I had the twins, I had a cleaning lady in my house once a week.

That meant that my house stayed organised exactly as I liked it 90% of the time.

We now have the twins plus a nanny in the house on a daily basis. My kitchen cupboards probably have to be tidied every week because of all the activity going on.

I don't organise every week but I do maintain, tweak and adjust things. If I expected my cupboards to stay tidy forever I might have been demotivated and disappointed in my initial efforts.

Do you see the difference?

2. Organise just enough

I feel that there is already way too much expected of women even before we add in the influences from the traditional and online media.

When we browse magazines and blogs, it's easy to think that the ideal is perfection.

Friends, perfection is overrated!

I'm here to tell you to get organised *just enough* so that you and your family both benefit, but not so much that you're trying to chase an unrealistic ideal, constantly comparing yourself to styled photo shoots in magazines and on blogs.

I hereby give you permission to relax and do *just enough*.

Don't you feel better already?

3. Determine your individual organising style

Each one of us has a different and unique personality.

Some of us like to pile and some of us like to file. Some of us like to plan and some of us like to fly by the seat of our pants.

There is no right way or wrong way; they're all just different styles.

It makes sense, then, for us to incorporate our personalities and styles into our organising endeavours.

If we don't, we run the risk of feeling like a failure because a solution that works perfectly for someone else doesn't work for us at all.

Why is it important to know your organising style?

- You can adapt your environment to support you instead of working against you
- You can prepare for challenges or obstacles before you even start

- You can get things done quicker because you're set up for success right from the start.

What is your organising style?

There are three distinct styles. Sometimes one is very prominent but more often than not, you can see one strong focus and a secondary sub-focus.

Style 1: Visual organiser

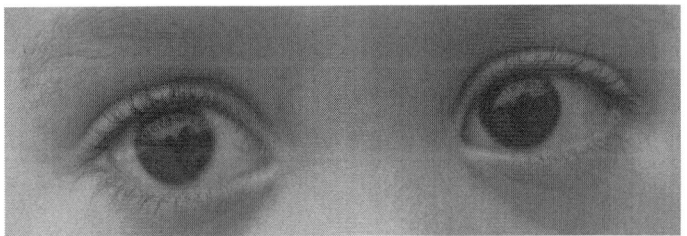

Characteristics of the visual organiser

- Primary sense for learning: **sight**
- Reads books or magazines, watches TV or surfs the internet/ blogs to relax.
- Remembers people's faces very easily but not necessarily their names.
- Learns by reading books, articles, etc.
- Tries to spell a difficult word by writing/ typing it out.

Organising tips for the visual organiser

- Out of sight, out of mind. If you don't see something, you'll forget to action it so keep things visible but neat.
- Label everything very clearly.
- Keep your desk tidy as you get distracted by a cluttered environment.
- Have only the paperwork that you are currently working with on your desk. Remove everything else.

- When trying to do computer work, close all windows on your computer, except the programme you're working on, but especially your email.

About 60% of people are visual learners.

Style 2: Auditory organiser

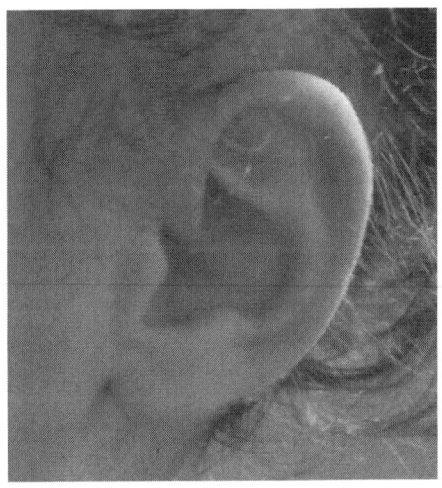

Characteristics of the auditory organiser

- Primary sense for learning: **hearing**

- Listens to the radio or music to relax.
- Remembers people's names but not their faces.
- Is easily distracted by noise when trying to work.
- Learns best by listening to audio downloads, CDs, etc.
- Tries to spell a difficult word by sounding it out.

Organising tips for the auditory organiser

- Forward your phone when you're trying to get important work done at the office
- Turn off your cell phone when you're mid-project.
- Turn off your computer's speakers and close your email so that you don't hear the beeps from incoming messages.

About 25% of people are auditory learners.

Style 3: Kinesthetic (tactile) organiser

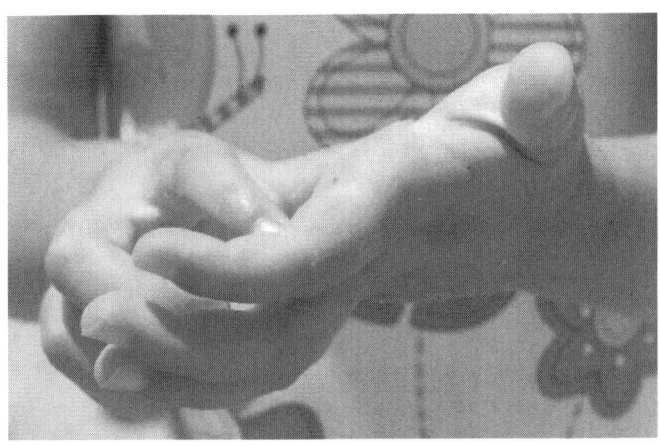

Characteristics of the kinesthetic (tactile) organiser

- Primary sense for learning: **doing**
- Plays sport, dances, goes to gym or does a physical activity to relax.

- Remembers people by what they did with that person. "Oh, that was the person we met at the movies."
- Is distracted by action and by people moving around.
- Learns by going to workshops, seminars, courses, etc.
- Tries to spell a difficult word by writing it out to see how it feels.

Organising tips for the kinesthetic organiser

- Make sure your desk faces away from people so you're not distracted by people moving around.
- Keep only those things you need on your desk as you're very likely to get distracted by playing with the stapler, paper clips, other papers, etc.
- Take regular breaks and move to keep focussed and on task.

About 15% of people are kinesthetic learners.

6. THREE PARTS TO GETTING AND STAYING ORGANISED

There are 3 steps to getting and staying organised:

1. Motivation
2. Skills
3. Accountability and support

Over the years of working with clients, I've found that lasting change doesn't happen unless all three elements are present.

Step one

Motivation

Whatever your reasons are for getting organised, make sure that you identify those reasons for yourself, so that when things start to get difficult, you can tap into that motivation and say, "I'm getting organised because of this reason, and this is why it's important to me".

1. Why do you want to get organised? This will mean different things for different people. No one way is the right answer.
2. What will it feel like when your home is organised?
3. What are you hoping to achieve by getting organised? More time, less stress, less cleaning, happier family?
4. Are you doing it for someone else? That's okay but better still is if you're also 100% sold on the idea.
5. Can you see the real life benefits for you and your family, or is it just some fad for you?
6. Do you have the unrealistic expectation that your home is going to look like something from an Oprah makeover show?
7. Are you committed to doing the work that will yield the results you want?

Go back and read the questions above and better still, take the time to consider them carefully and answer them.

Step two

Skills

I know there are some schools of thought that say you're either born organised or you're not.

There is some truth to that but I do know that every person can learn the skills to be organised.

Like most skills, the more you practise the better you get. And the better you get the more you enjoy doing it.

Over the next couple of chapters, I'll teach you my D R E A M method of getting and staying organised.

Step three

Accountability and support

This is the crucial and often missing third step.

Once you're organised, it's very, very easy to lapse back into disorder if you have no support from family or friends or the accountability needed to effect lasting change.

Imagine that you've just worked hard on your pantry for four hours decluttering and throwing out old food, organising and labelling shelves and everything finally is all done.

You then go grocery shopping and your kids pack the food any which way.

It's enough to demotivate even the most motivated of organisers.

This is why it's so important to have your family's **support** as you embark on your organising journey.

If you have an organised friend or a friend who also needs to get organised, that person will be great to keep you accountable. Otherwise, there are tons of blogs out there.

Pick one or two that you like and when the blogger posts a project, do it in your home the very next weekend. Once you get into a regular accountability habit, it'll become easier to keep up with it.

This is why I love blogging – I see it as an opportunity for me to constantly be challenged and kept on my toes because I know I have to share some organising tips every week.

Let's look at a few scenarios:

Scenario 1

Andrew is married to Jane. He keeps complaining that the house is disorderly and he can't relax at home.

Jane finally decides to get organised to keep Andrew happy.

This change is not likely to be a lasting change because she intends to get organised solely for him.

Scenario 2

Susan and her kids get into shouting matches every morning as they all get ready for school and work because one or more of the kids can't find their school clothes, bags, books, etc. One morning she decides that enough is enough; she's going to get organised.

In this scenario, Susan has tapped into her motivation. She now needs to learn how to put systems into place to sort out the early morning rush.

Scenario 3

Mary can't understand why she can't keep her home organised. She reads about 10 organising blogs, gets good ideas on a regular basis and best of all, regularly tries to do some organising projects. Yet, nothing stays organised.

Mary is clearly motivated and has learnt some skills but lacks the maintenance and support to keep her home organised.

There are bits and pieces of Jane, Susan and Mary in each of us.

We all get inspired by organised spaces and the key is to take that **inspiration** and move us to **action**.

7. DREAM METHOD FOR GETTING AND STAYING ORGANISED

D – Decide on your vision for the space

The first step in organising any space is to ask yourself these 3 questions:

1. What is my vision for this space?
2. What is this space going to be used for?
3. What do I want this space to feel like?

Examples

Your desk

1. What is my vision for this space?

No clutter, everything in its place, can find things easily

2. What is this space going to be used for? Computer work, weekly menu planning and scrapbooking

3. What do I want this space to feel like? Neat, inspiring, organised

Your children's bedroom

1. What is my vision for this space? No clutter, clear zones, representative of their personalities

2. What is this space going to be used for? Sleeping, reading, dressing

3. What do I want this space to feel like?
    Comfortable, relaxing, a sanctuary

It takes a few extra minutes to answer these questions upfront but is very valuable down the road.

For example, when you're organising your children's bedroom and you find toys in there, you go back to your dream for that space.

Are the kids supposed to be playing there?

No. They play in a playroom so the toys will therefore have to be removed and taken to the playroom.

See? Knowing your vision helps with decision-making.

R - Remove everything and clean (if necessary)

When you remove everything from a space you want to organise, you can see exactly the amount of space you have to work with and also what you have that you no longer need.

If necessary, clean the space. At the very least, wipe shelves down with a clean cloth.

It's easier to see what you want in a space when you start off with a clean slate.

If you try to start organising without removing everything first, not much really changes. But when you start with an empty slate, you can purposefully decide what you do want to add to the space.

Now that the space is empty, what does that feel like for you? Does it leave you with a feeling of peace and tranquility, or do you feel anxious at the emptiness? Why do you think that is so?

E - Eliminate the clutter

You can't organise clutter. Before you can organise anything, you need to get rid of anything that shouldn't be there.

Marcia's definition of clutter – anything you don't love or use, or that serves you in any way.

Let's look at each of those clutter components.

Things you don't love

Many of us keep things around that we don't like because we've been given them as gifts, we paid a lot of money for it or it's become a habit.

Gifts

Once something has been gifted to you, it is then yours to do with whatever you want.

If you don't like it and will use it, give it to someone else or donate it. I used to get a lot of bath goodies for birthdays and Christmas. Lovely idea and I'm always very grateful but I bath maybe 10 times a year, if that. So I regift or donate to an orphanage my church supports.

We spent a lot of money

Not all sale items are good deals if you don't need them. Sometimes an item of clothing looks like a good deal but then once you fit on said item at home, it looks horrendous on you. You can't return it so it stays in your wardrobe.

Why?

Your clothes should make you look and feel fabulous.

I once bought an absolutely gorgeous suede jacket. The colour was perfect for me and the size was right so I bought it.

The only problem is that every time I wore this jacket, I'd be so aware that it was about 5 cm shorter than what I'm comfortable wearing.

I wore this jacket on and off for about a year because I loved the colour but eventually I decided that it would look *even more* fabulous on someone else and so I gave it away.

Don't hang onto old habits

Many of us have things in our home that we haven't looked at with a fresh eye in years.

Once we put things out and we're reasonably happy with them, we leave them there and they become part of the furniture.

Maybe there's a vase you used to like but your taste has changed?

Or maybe you were gifted something and used it for a while, fully intending to remove it, but you forgot about it and it's now part of your decorating habits.

We were gifted a lamp that was never to my taste but because we had very little furniture, we used it for a number of years.

When we could afford to get our own furniture, we still never thought about replacing this lamp until recently. And that's only because I went around my house with "fresh eyes" looking to see where I could freshen up the look of our home.

Things you don't use

My rule of thumb is this: if I haven't used it for about 6 – 12 months, chances are the item is seasonal (like Christmas decorations) or I don't need it.

Store your seasonal decorations and items you use only once a year in hard-to-reach places so that they don't take up prime real estate.

We only entertain big groups of people three times a year – at Christmas, for the twins' birthday and for our birthday. My husband and I celebrate our birthdays over a 10-day period so we have one celebration on the weekend between the two birthdays. Yes, it is very convenient.

All my extra plates, mugs and cutlery are stored in the sideboard in the dining room so that they're out of the way.

Are you holding onto things just in case you might need them someday?

I used to do this all the time until I had a revelation.

Somebody could use these things today.

Whenever I'm tempted to hang onto things just in case, I remind myself that there are plenty of people who could use those things today instead of them taking up valuable real estate in my home.

Let go of things you don't need – it's incredibly freeing living a simpler life.

Things that don't serve you

There are some things that you don't use but that do serve you.

They might not be functional but they are pretty and make you happy.

Keep them. Life is too short not to be inspired.

Some of my clients over the years have written me beautiful cards to thank me for working with them and for making a difference in their lives.

I have two of those cards framed and on my desk.

Technically, they're not of any use but they do make me very happy and inspire me when I feel demotivated and need my spirits lifted.

Are you sentimental?

I am not usually a very sentimental person but I do have some ideas to declutter while still holding onto some sentimental items.

1. Keep a memory box

With letters, cards and notes, I restrict myself to a **memory box** which, in my house, is the size of a large shoebox.

When that box gets too full, I make myself go through it to throw out things that are no longer as meaningful for me. It's amazing to me how something that you absolutely had to keep at the time can lose its sentimental value after a few years.

2. Take a picture of the item.

I've found success in taking pics of sentimental items and then letting them go. I go one step further and blog about it so that I can record my feelings and thoughts. You could do the same or keep a mini scrapbook album to preserve the memories but let go of the clutter.

3. Hold the memory not the stuff.

Just because you let go of things doesn't mean you love the person any less.

Remember that when you have fewer things, each becomes more meaningful to you. If you have just one item from a family member who died, it is much easier to honour that item rather than a box of stuff.

Let's look at my definition of clutter again.

Anything you don't love or use, or that serves you in any way

Everything else is clutter and should go.

If you have difficulty in getting rid of things, I'd encourage you to keep some things in a special container, label it with the date and look at those things again in 6 months. You may feel more detached then.

I've just gone through this exercise with some really smart work suits. I let go of some very easily and there were about 10 that I was only able to let go of this very week.

A – Arrange in a way that works for you

This is the part that people actually think of when they think about organising. I want to point out something to you. This is only step 4 in a 5-step process.

Can you now see how important it is to get the other 3 steps done first and *then* get to the actual organising?

Arrange means to position things better. To assemble things into different groups, to put together, to sort and so on.

Gather 4 large boxes or bins for throwing away, giving away, moving to a different area and keeping.

Box 1: Throw away

This box is for actual trash, things that are broken and beyond repair or things that you would feel ashamed to donate to someone.

For organising paper, you would throw away appliance manuals of appliances you no longer own, expired receipts, recipes you don't want to try, notes you no longer need, etc.

Remember to shred paper with identifying information to reduce the risk of personal identification fraud.

Box 2: Give away

This box is for anything that may still be useful to someone else. You can either donate or sell these items.

A cautionary note on selling things – sometimes selling is more trouble than it's worth. Your time is a lot more valuable than just a couple of Rands or Dollars.

If you're going to the trouble of selling your items, make sure you have a big enough batch of things that people actually want to buy or that the items are high value.

Don't waste your time on low-value items – rather donate these to an orphanage or women's shelter. I guarantee you'll feel better about the experience and they will too!

We used to sell all our books back to a second hand bookshop for many years because we'd get really good deals. Something changed in their management and they now pay peanuts for the same, excellent quality books (both my husband and I are fanatical about keeping books in excellent condition).

We now donate our books to a charity shop near our home. They sell the items to make money for a home for mentally disabled people. It's a win-win situation – they get really excellent stuff and we get the satisfaction of feeling good.

Box 3: Move to a different area

This box is for anything that is not meant for the current space you're organising.

We know it's not meant for the space because it doesn't fall into the dream or the vision for that space as we decided in step 1 of our DREAM method.

You could physically take the items to the room they belong in but I prefer using the box for a number of reasons:

- It saves time to move those items all at once
- It prevents you from getting distracted as you return things to their rightful places

1. **Box 4: Keep**

This is the only pile that we will actually organise.

If you've been ruthless in decluttering, typically this pile will be about half of what you had in the space at first.

How to organise the fourth box, your "keep" pile

Big items first

It's always a good idea to put the larger items into the space first and then nestle the smaller pieces later.

Store like items together

If you're organising a stationery drawer, keep all the pens, staples, paper clips, Post-It pads together. Don't have one section with staples, paper clips and push pins all together. That makes no sense and will frustrate you when you need a paper clip and keep extracting staples.

Use containers

Containers help to keep things neat and ordered. They also help to provide boundaries to prevent excess. If you have a box for all your glue sticks and the box is full, do you really need more? Probably not.

1. Use square or rectangular containers

I love using straight-edged containers to save space. Yes, round ones may be cute but they are not the best use of small spaces.

I have one exception – Styrofoam disposable cups can be squished into small spaces without breaking!

2. Use see-through containers

Opaque containers (with labels) are great if you want to present a uniform look and feel. In the kitchen I prefer see-through containers. They allow you to see exactly what you have and prevent wastage of food items.

Use labels

Label liberally especially if you or a couple of your family members are visual people. Also use labels for any closed boxes or opaque containers.

You don't need a label-maker unless you really want one; use sticky labels or even masking tape with a permanent marker. Masking tape is my favourite labelling tool, especially in the kitchen. If you want to get fancier, you can write on washi tape and use the tape as labels.

Keep it simple

Simple systems = organising SUCCESS

Easy, simple systems mean people are more likely to use them and thus spell success.

If your family members don't put their clothes in a closed laundry hamper, try leaving the top off and see the difference. It's about making things easy to use for everybody concerned.

M – Maintain the space

This is the most important organising step ever.

When you clean something, you don't expect it to stay clean forever. You know that the minute you're done with breakfast, there are breakfast dishes. Those have to be washed, dried and packed away. Then lunch comes around and you have to repeat the whole process.

And again for supper.

Cleaning is never-ending.

Organising is similar but thankfully, not as bad.

You're likely to spend quite a bit of time on your first organising attempt of any space. When you go back and tweak things that don't quite work for you, it will then only take a short time.

Please know that you can't expect to organise once and never do it again. That is unrealistic and will set you up for failure.

Remember...

- Other people also use the same space
- You're buying or getting new things all the time
- Your life is changing – you get busier at work, move house, kids outgrow their clothes, systems no longer work, etc.

I can tell you why maintenance is important by this old saying: **a stitch in time saves nine.**

If you keep maintaining, you only use a few minutes.

When you let it get totally out of hand, it takes hours.

Here are four ideas for maintaining your organised space:

Idea 1

Do a quick, 5-minute room rescue every night, or a 1-hour rescue every week

Depending on how big your house is and how out of control it gets during the day, do a quick pick up and tidy of between 5 – 15 minutes every evening.

I do the same with my study. I like to have a clean desk to work at every day so I take an extra minute returning pens to the holder, putting notebooks in my desk drawers, returning books to the bookshelf, and so on. It sometimes feels cumbersome but I remind myself of how nice it will be to walk into the room the following day.

Idea 2

One in, one out: for clothes, home ware, computer documents, etc.

I'm certainly not saying that at the very minute you walk into your house with a new shopping bag, you declutter your wardrobe and remove exactly what you bought – one pair of jeans, two tops and a pair of shoes.

But... take the time as soon as you can (I like to do it on the weekend following the purchase) to go through and declutter a few things.

In the kitchen, when I know I want to get a new frying pan, etc, I like to declutter first so that the space is ready for my new item.

Also take the time to go through your computer documents at least once a month, but preferably once a week. Again, if you do this weekly (although not always possible), it is much quicker, usually just a few minutes as opposed to at least an hour once a month.

Idea 3

Assign a home for absolutely everything

Before you buy, think about where that item will go. Get in the habit of making prompt decisions because indecision equals clutter.

At times during the year when lots of items typically come into the home (birthdays and Christmas), keep them in a central place for a day or two while you decide where they will go.

Don't just stash them in the nearest cupboard without being intentional about it.

Idea 4

Establish limits and set boundaries

This is the best way to maintain your space.

Limits and boundaries help to take away some of the decision-making.

Some of my limits and boundary examples are:

1. Once my one magazine rack is full, any extra magazines must go.
2. I only keep three copies of each magazine.
3. Once my file folder is full, I will not move to a second one – I have to declutter.
4. All my inspirational ideas have to fit into one project folder.
5. I will only keep as many books as can fit onto my bookshelf in a neat and organised manner.

8. MY FAVOURITE ORGANISING PRINCIPLES

These principles were certainly not invented by me but I can say that these are the ones I talk about the most.

1. A place for everything and everything in its place

Have a designated place for every single thing, especially before you buy it. While you're still in the store, ask yourself, "where will this go?" and if you don't know, don't buy it. Once you decide where it will go, you can go back and get it. Yes, you might miss out a couple of things but rather that than a cluttered and overcrowded home.

Everything in your house should have a *specific home*. The goal should be that if anyone asks, "where do I find the _____?" you should be able to tell them immediately.

2. One in, one out

We spoke about this principle in the maintenance step of the DREAM organising process. It's so important that it bears repeating.

It really is the easiest way to keep the clutter under control and a great reminder to continually declutter.

The rule is definitely one in, one out. But even better is one in, two out.

3. Store items where they are used

Store coffee mugs near the kettle and plates near the stove. In other words, keep things where you use them. If you use scissors in the kitchen, bathroom and study, then have a pair in each room.

Not only does this make practical sense, but it saves you time too.

One of my favourite *really easy* organising tips is to have a bin in each room of your home. You'll be surprised at how much time you save walking from room to room.

4. Write everything down

A blunt pencil is better than a sharp mind. The key to an organised mind is getting it all down. You don't have to get fancy; a plain and simple lined notebook will do just fine. That said, if gorgeous and luxurious notebooks are going to inspire you to actually use them, then fancy up!

I have notebooks in my car, in the kitchen, in the study, in my handbag and even on my bedside table. I like spiral-bound notebooks for this purpose so I can rip out the pages and go.

5. Plan your life

Set aside time every weekend to plan your activities, events and meals for the week ahead. Before you finish up your work for the day, take 5 minutes to quickly plan your main priority tasks for the next day.
When you get in the habit of planning your life, you'll wonder how you ever got along without it.

6. Don't put it down; put it away

This tip is from my dear friend, Suzanne Babb, in Arizona, and I love it.

When you walk into a room with something, don't just dump it anywhere. Put it away in its designated place. It takes a few seconds longer but is so worth the time saving in the long run.

7. Set up and keep simple systems

A system tells you what to do when something happens. For instance, as you run low or finish foods, they immediately go on your shopping list. That's a system. Weekly menu planning is another system.

When the laundry basket in the bedroom is full, the clothes get emptied into the washing machine. That's another system.

Morning and evening routines are also example of systems.

8. Use every minute

We often wait until we have an hour to tackle a project. Don't wait. Use 5, 10 or 15 minutes whenever you can find some time.

A few minutes a day in each of your major areas equals an organised life.

I like to have a list (sometimes only mental) of things I can do in 5, 10 and 15-minute blocks. In 5 minutes, I can do any one of these tasks: reply to 2 to 3 emails, tidy my desk, fold some clothes, put on a pot of rice or phone a friend.

Let go of the perfectionism that says you need to anything perfectly or not at all.

9. SET UP YOUR ROUTINES FOR SUCCESS

I used to hate the word routine because I thought it sounded boring.

The truth is that routines help you to have some flow or rhythm to your days.

When you know what your evening routine needs to look like, you can get that done quickly and then relax knowing that you're prepared for the next day.

When you know what your morning routine looks like, you can start your day on the right foot instead of rushed, stressed and frazzled.

Example of a weekend routine

- Do a load of laundry
- Make menu plan for the week
- Draw up grocery list

- Do grocery shopping
- Do some batch cooking
- Go to the library

Here's how you set up your routines:

1. Make a list of everything that needs to happen for your home and life to run smoothly.
2. All these things don't necessarily need to be done by you. Everybody should pitch in and even little kids should have age-appropriate chores.
3. Next to each routine, write D, W or M for daily, weekly or monthly for the frequency of the task.
4. List all of the daily, weekly and monthly tasks on separate lists.
5. For the daily ones, decide which have to be done in the morning and which can be done in the evening.

Keep tweaking your routines until they comfortably fit your life.

Part 3

Beyond getting organised

10. AVOID THESE ORGANISING MISTAKES

Buying containers first

Remember you'll typically declutter 25 – 50% of your stuff first so save money by buying containers last

Thinking your efforts have to look pretty to be effective

Does it work for you or your family? Then it's effective.

It does help you to want to maintain the space if it's pretty but it's not necessary.

Thinking organising is a once-off event and not a journey

Just like cleaning, organising is an ongoing event. You're going to have to tweak, maintain and re-organise now and again.

Getting caught up in organising and not enjoying the results

When you start to care more about how pretty your cupboards look than the fact your kids want to help, something has gone wrong.

Remember organising is a means to an end (an enjoyable and stress-free life) and not the end.

11. GREEN ORGANISING

I think it's the responsible thing to do to try and be as green as possible when organising by doing what you can to protect our environment.

Let's talk about three actions: reuse, recycle and repurpose.

1. Reuse

- Cut notepads from any paper that is only printed on one side and use the reverse for scrap paper for you or your kids.

- If you receive plastic bags from stores, reuse those bags over and over again.

- We even reuse our bread and cereal bags.

- Use fabric shopping bags. Keep some in your car(s) or near the door so that you never have to remember them – you're automatically setting yourself up for success.

2. Recycle

When you're decluttering paper, collect it all for your city's paper recycling project. If your city/ town doesn't have a convenient collection system, you may have to find out where you can drop off your paper.

In my city, we're fortunate in that we get bags to place outside every week for collection.

Glass, plastic and other materials can and also should be recycled.

Caution – don't get so hung up on the recycling that you start hoarding. Set up an easy weekly system to get the recycling out of your home.

3. Repurpose

Cereal boxes

- Cut off about 10 cm to use as dividers in your underwear and sock drawers, or in your junk drawer.
- Trim off the top of the cereal box at an angle, cover it with paper to match your décor and you have beautiful magazine holders.

Glass jars

- Glass jars can be used to store stationery items like paper clips and staples, to buttons, ribbon and thread in your craft room.
- I also store my various teas in glass jars in the kitchen.
- When the labels are washed off, they are extremely appealing visually. Remember to store like with like though.

Ice cream containers

- In your kids' bedroom, use to store small toys like Lego, matchbox cars, crayons, etc.
- In the kitchen, use to store packets of sauce or gravy, or boxes of soup.
- Also use in the fridge as mini drawers to keep different types of food separate, e.g. lunch meats and cheeses, sandwich vegetables, etc. The best thing about this idea is that if there are food spills, you need only clean the container, and not the entire fridge.

IN CLOSING

Remember what I said at the start of this book?

The goal is to be organised just enough so your family and life functions well.

The goal is not to have a "perfect" home, if such a thing even exists

If helping you get organised saves you just 10 minutes every day, I'll consider this book a success.

But more than that, I want you to have the peace that being organised brings.

Love and organising success

Marcia Francois

Part 4

15 tools to organise your home and life

1. My future organised home
2. Plan your attack
3. Master to do list
4. Projects to do in 15 minutes
5. Projects to do in 1 hour
6. My routines
7. Grocery list
8. Goals form – category
9. Goals form – blank
10. Eat the frog
11. Monthly planner
12. Monthly menu planner
13. Priority list
14. Health chart
15. Travel checklist

You can also download PDFs of these forms from my website at

http://www.liveorganised.com/p/downloads.html

My Future Organised Home

Remember that the biggest motivator to action is always a big enough why. So take a few moments and picture your **future organised life**. We are all different so this will mean different things for each of us.

Describe what you see in the space below.

_____
_____
_____
_____
_____
_____
_____
_____

Which organisational areas concern you the most? List the top areas.

_____
_____
_____
_____
_____
_____
_____
_____
_____
_____
_____

Plan your attack

1. Write the name of the room or space in the centre circle
2. Mind map the different areas that need organising

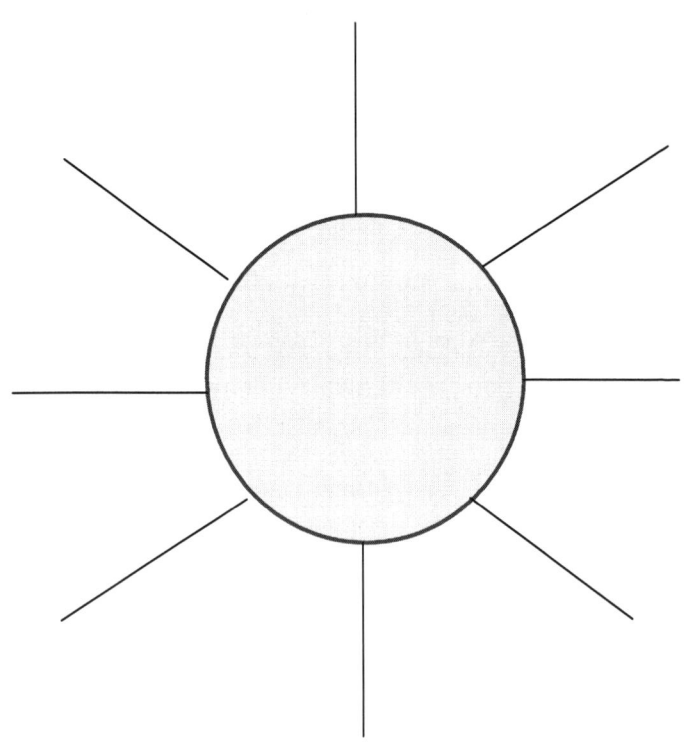

My PRIORITISED action steps are as follows:

No.	Action step	Date
1		
2		
3		
4		
5		
6		
7		
8		
9		
10		
11		
12		
13		
14		
15		

Master "to do" list

No.	What do I need to do?	Due by?	Done
1			
2			
3			
4			
5			
6			
7			
8			
9			
10			
11			
12			
13			
14			
15			

Projects to do in 15 minutes

No.	Details	Date
1		
2		
3		
4		
5		
6		
7		
8		
9		
10		
11		
12		
13		
14		
15		
16		

Projects to do in 1 hour

No.	Details	Date
1		
2		
3		
4		
5		
6		
7		
8		
9		
10		
11		
12		
13		
14		
15		
16		

My routines

Laminate this sheet and stick it up somewhere. Then use a whiteboard marker to list and cross off items on a daily or weekly basis.

Morning

☐ _____
☐ _____
☐ _____
☐ _____

Afternoon/ Evening

☐ _____
☐ _____
☐ _____
☐ _____

Weekly

☐ _____
☐ _____
☐ _____
☐ _____

Monthly

☐ _____
☐ _____
☐ _____

Grocery list

Dairy	Bakery	Fruits & Veggies
_____	_____	_____
_____	_____	_____
_____	_____	_____
_____	_____	_____

Frozen Foods	Meats	Fridge/Deli
_____	_____	_____
_____	_____	_____
_____	_____	_____
_____	_____	_____

Dry goods	Cans	Condiments
_____	_____	_____
_____	_____	_____
_____	_____	_____
_____	_____	_____

My goals for _____

1	Spiritual
2	Family
3	Work/ Career
4	Ministry
5	Health & fitness
6	Social
7	Personal/ rest & relaxation

My goals for _____

1	
2	
3	
4	
5	
6	
7	

Eat the frog

Every day, list 3 tasks that you need to do, in order of priority. Work on the tasks in order until your list is done.

Monday	Done?

Tuesday	Done?

Wednesday	Done?

Thursday	Done?

Friday	Done?

Monthly planner _____

No.	What?	Where?	Time?
1			
2			
3			
4			
5			
6			
7			
8			
9			
10			
11			
12			
13			
14			
15			
16			
17			
18			
19			
20			
21			
22			
23			
24			
25			
26			
27			
28			
29			
30			
31			

Monthly menu planner _____

Day	Meal	Notes
1		
2		
3		
4		
5		
6		
7		
8		
9		
10		
11		
12		
13		
14		
15		
16		
17		
18		
19		
20		
21		
22		
23		
24		
25		
26		
27		
28		
29		
30		
31		

Monthly priority list _____

No.	Spiritual	Done?
1		
2		
3		

No.	Family	Done?
1		
2		
3		

No.	Work/ Business	Done?
1		
2		
3		

No.	Health and fitness	Done?
1		
2		
3		

No.	Self-care	Done?
1		
2		
3		

No.	Financial	Done?
1		
2		
3		

Health chart   Month: _____

Day	Weight	Exercise	Water	Fruit	Vegetables
1					
2					
3					
4					
5					
6					
7					
8					
9					
10					
11					
12					
13					
14					
15					
16					
17					
18					
19					
20					
21					
22					
23					
24					
25					
26					
27					
28					
29					
30					
31					

Travel checklist

Clothes

- ☐ Underwear
- ☐ PJ's
- ☐ Jeans
- ☐ Tracksuit
- ☐ Sweatshirts
- ☐ Long-sleeved tops
- ☐ T-shirts
- ☐ Shorts
- ☐ Jerseys
- ☐ Jacket

Shoes

- ☐ Boots/ smart shoes
- ☐ Sports shoes
- ☐ Sandals

Beach wear

- ☐ Costume
- ☐ Beach towel
- ☐ Cap

Travelling stuff

- ☐ Camera & cables
- ☐ Sunglasses
- ☐ Cell phone

Toiletries

- ☐ Shampoo
- ☐ Conditioner
- ☐ Brush & comb
- ☐ Toothpaste
- ☐ Toothbrush
- ☐ Dental floss
- ☐ Soap/ shower gel
- ☐ Body lotion
- ☐ Talc
- ☐ Deodorant
- ☐ Makeup

Medicinal

- ☐ Vitamins
- ☐ Painkillers
- ☐ Cold/ flu tablets
- ☐ Sunblock
- ☐ Plasters

Other

- ☐ Umbrella
- ☐ Batteries
- ☐ Hair dryer
- ☐ Bible
- ☐ Books/ Kindle
- ☐ Lip ice
- ☐ Hand cream

ABOUT THE AUTHOR

Marcia Francois is a time management coach and speaker in Johannesburg, South Africa, who inspires busy women to break out of overwhelm, make the most of their time and take purposeful and focussed action so they have the time and freedom to live life to the full.

She also works full-time, is a wife to Dion and a mother to sassy, boy/ girl twin toddlers, Connor and Kendra.

Visit Marcia online at www.liveorganised.com or www.OrganisingQueen.com

5119754R00059

Printed in Great Britain
by Amazon.co.uk, Ltd.,
Marston Gate.